# CIM REVISION CARDS

## Strategic Marketing Decisions

Mike Willoughby of Marketing Knowledge

**ELSEVIER**

BUTTERWORTH
HEINEMANN

AMSTERDAM • BOSTON • HEIDELBERG • LONDON • NEW YORK • OXFORD
PARIS • SAN DIEGO • SAN FRANCISCO • SINGAPORE • SYDNEY • TOKYO

Butterworth-Heinemann is an imprint of Elsevier
Linacre House, Jordan Hill, Oxford OX2 8DP
30 Corporate Drive, Suite 400, Burlington, MA 01803

First published 2006

**British Library Cataloguing in Publication Data**
A catalogue record for this book is available from the British Library

**Library of Congress Cataloguing in Publication Data**
A catalogue record for this book is available from the Library of Congress

ISBN-13: 978-0-7506-6767-8
ISBN-10: 0-7506-6767-8

For information on all Butterworth-Heinemann publications visit our web site at http://books.elsevier.com

Printed and bound in Great Britain

05 06 07 08 09 10   10 9 8 7 6 5 4 3 2 1

# TABLE OF CONTENTS

# PREFACE

Welcome to the CIM Revision Cards from Elsevier/Butterworth–Heinemann. We hope you will find these useful to revise for your CIM exam. The cards are designed to be used in conjunction with the CIM Coursebooks from Elsevier/Butterworth–Heinemann, and have been written specifically with revision in mind. They also serve as invaluable reviews of the complete modules, perfect for those studying via the assignment route.

- Learning outcomes at the start of each chapter identify the main points
- Key topics are summarized, helping you commit the information to memory quickly and easily
- Examination and revision tips are provided to give extra guidance when preparing for the exam
- Key diagrams are featured to aid the learning process
- The compact size ensures the cards are easily transportable, so you can revise any time, anywhere

To get the most of your revision cards, try to look over them as frequently as you can when taking your CIM course. When read alongside the Coursebook they serve as the ideal companion to the main text. Good luck – we wish you every success with your CIM qualification!

# INTRODUCTION TO STRATEGIC MARKETING DECISIONS

**Unit 1**

## KEY DEFINITIONS

**A stakeholder** – is anyone who has an interest in or an impact on an organization's activities.

**Strategic marketing decisions** – are the decisions made as part of the iterative process of strategy development. A company makes these decisions in response to the changing dimensions of the marketing environment in order to ensure a sustainable competitive advantage. Strategic marketing decisions are part of the problem solving process and are required throughout the process of analysis, strategic choice and implementation.

**A sustainable competitive advantage** – is the achievement of a company to develop a superior, differentiated position in the market place which creates superior value for customers, shareholders and stakeholders and which they are able to maintain over a period of time.

**Hard-edged marketing** – is the process by which marketing managers ensure they make decisions that create superior value for all stakeholders, especially customers and shareholders, and prove the value of marketing's contribution to business by the use of meaningful marketing metrics.

**Market/competitive lifecycles** – describe the cyclical nature of the demand and competitive activity in markets. Lifecycles are based on the notion that during the life time of a market, it passes through a number of distinct phases, each of which has particular characteristics with regard to the nature of competitor activity, the demand for a product and the type of strategies that are appropriate to meet the distinct characteristics of the phase.

# The evolution of marketing thinking

From a long-term perspective, marketing has developed through four stages of thinking. Taking a shorter term view, marketing managers and decision makers have to respond to five priorities.

## Stages of marketing thinking (Doyle, 2000)

- Transactional Marketing – focusing on short term profits

- Brand Marketing – building customer loyalty by building an attachment, emotional or otherwise, between the customer and the brand

- Relationship marketing – building customer loyalty and retention through a wider range of approaches

- Value-based marketing – building value to shareholders by delivering a total value proposition to an organization's customers

## Five priorities for decision makers (Wilson and Gilligan, 2004)

- The pace of change and the need to respond with innovative solutions

- Fragmented markets and the increased need to customize

- Superior customer value as a basic ingredient of competitiveness

- Information, market knowledge and the ability to learn as a source of competitive advantage

- The strategic significance of new types of partnerships and new networks of relationships in the supply chain

# The changing dimensions of competitive advantage – the role of lifecycles

The bases of competitive advantage are continually changing as the environment changes. These changes are influenced by a number of lifecycles, which will vary across the world. This variance poses both an opportunity and challenge for strategic decision makers.

**The Market/Industry Lifecycle** has four distinct stages moving from little concentration through emergence of competition, specialization, and, finally, to consolidation and withdrawal

**Demand/Technology Lifecycles** consist of the demand lifecycle which is the underlying need within the market whilst the technology lifecycle deals with the ways in which this need is satisfied

**The Competitive Lifecycle** dictates that pioneers who achieve first mover advantage are challenged by competitors, leading to a diminishing opportunity for premium pricing and, ultimately, commodity competition

# How organizations compete to achieve customer preference

Treacy and Wiersma (1995) propose four focuses by which companies may achieve customer preferences:

**Operational Excellence** – Companies compete not by technological innovation but by targeting a customer preference for value for money

**Customer Intimacy** – Companies can target on an individual basis through mass customization of both products and marketing

**Product Leadership** – Companies focus on developing products that push at the boundaries of innovation, making high investments in research and development

**Brand Leadership** – Companies base their strategic position on brand leadership supported by the extra value proposition created by the brand

## The role of competitive relationships

An integral part of many companies' strategy is to form relationships with competitors in order to achieve sustainable competitive advantage. The driving forces for this trend are:

- Companies do not have **sufficient resources** alone to realize their full global potential and so may form a relationship to achieve better operational excellence or perhaps greater customer intimacy
- The **pace of innovation and market diffusion** is ever more rapid and so, to achieve global brand leadership, relationships may be formed so that new products and services can be exploited quickly by effective diffusion into the global market
- **High R&D costs** mean it is increasingly difficult, costly and risky for companies to develop breakthrough innovations alone. Thus to achieve product leadership, relationships may be formed in R&D as in the Sony/Philips alliance, which produced the new mini disc player
- In **mature markets** such as the car and airline industries, operational excellence has been achieved by the formation of alliances, mergers and takeovers to rationalize competition, achieve economies of scale and so achieve cost leadership in the industry
- Some companies use relationships to acquire the capability **to access new markets** where they have little expertise or experience so they are better positioned to compete for customer preference in those markets

## Revision tips

- It is important to understand the way in which lifecycles develop across the world, leading to differing conditions in different countries and regions. These lead to differing bases of competitive advantage which themselves are continually changing as the lifecycles continue to develop

- In order to avoid strategic drift, organizations have to take account of the changing bases of competitive advantage and review and develop their strategies accordingly

- Finally, Strategic Marketing Decisions need to be implemented and this implementation requires a carefully designed project plan with clear objectives and management skills appropriate to the project

# CHALLENGING TRADITIONAL STRATEGIC THINKING

Unit 2

➡ Examine the significance and application of new marketing thinking to strategic decisions

➡ Determine drivers for realignment in strategic thinking

➡ Explore the alternative approaches to strategic marketing decisions

➡ Examine issues in strategic marketing decision making in SMEs

➡ Explain and evaluate the contribution of value-based marketing

**Syllabus Reference: 2.1, 2.5, 2.6, 2.10, 4.1**

## Traditional strategic thinking

There are two interpretations of this phrase, both of which are valid to consider:

■ **Traditional thinking within organizations.** 'This is the way we have always done things'. As markets and economies move through their lifecycles, the bases of competitive advantage are likely to change. Organizations have, therefore, to consider how they should respond.

■ **Traditional methods of developing strategy.** As the pace of change increases so a premium is put on the ability of organizations to adapt to change. Approaches that are more organic and flexible than traditional linear approaches have, therefore, to be considered.

## KEY DEFINITIONS

**Breakpoints** – Occur in markets as a consequence of a major change in the environment or the competitive nature of the market which results in a previously successful strategy being made obsolete.

**Value-based marketing** – A marketing strategy that is based on a totally integrated marketing effort which delivers superior value to customers and so in turn delivers superior value to shareholders.

**Shareholder value principle** – The shareholder value principle asserts that marketing strategies should be judged by the economic returns they generate for shareholders, the returns being measured by dividends and increases in the company share price.

**Emergent strategies** – A strategy that has been developed through an iterative learning process so that the resultant strategy is one that has emerged through the creative and iterative process of crafting a strategy of proactively seeking new opportunities whilst reacting to the challenges faced in the market.

# Drivers for realignment in strategic thinking

There are a number of important environmental factors that give rise to four important drivers for strategic alignment.

## Issues/Environmental Factors

- Increasing globalization of the marketplace
- Emergence of the global village
- Growth and movement of populations across the globe
- Growing body of international law
- Piracy
- Shrinking communications
- The internet and access to the world wide web

## Emergent needs

- Rising customer expectations
- The drive for increased revenue and growth from the marketplace
- The intensification of global competition
- The need for innovation and creativity

## Application of new marketing thinking to strategic decisions

### The need for innovative thinking

Wilson and Gilligan (2004) suggest that changes in the marketing environment create breakpoints for the following reasons:

■ Changes in demographics or social structure

■ Technological breakthroughs

■ The identification of new business opportunities which redefine the market

■ Shifts within the distribution network leading to changes in power balances and consequent changes in expectations

■ Indirect competitors becoming direct competitors by developing new capabilities

■ Maturity of markets forcing rethinks in the face of declining returns

Piercy (2002) states that this leads to the need for strategic decisions to be concerned with:

■ How to create value

■ How to harness the power and impact of the internet, particularly in relation to channel decisions

■ How to achieve a totally integrated marketing effort to create customer value

■ How to engender creativity within an organization and avoid the bureaucracy associated with formal planning

## Application of new marketing thinking to strategic decisions

### The need to deliver shareholder value

Doyle (2000) suggests that,

*The key to creating shareholder value is building relationships with target customers based on satisfying their needs more effectively than competitors*

■ The shareholder value principle asserts that marketing strategies should be judged by the increase in value that they generate for the company based on the net present value of the income and expenditure streams together with the change in value of the company. Two principles then apply:

◇ The primary obligation of managers is to maximize returns for shareholders and owners

◇ The stock market value of a company (the market capitalization) is based on the investors' expectations of the cash generating abilities of the company

Doyle further states that delivering Value Based Marketing requires:

■ A deep understanding of customer needs

■ The formulation of value propositions that create differential advantage in meeting these needs

■ Building long-term relationships with customers

■ An understanding that the delivery of superior value is based on superior knowledge, systems, skills and marketing assets

## Alternative approaches to strategic marketing decisions

There are clear differences between the rational formal approach and the emergent strategy approach to decision making.

### Rational Formal Approach

- Linear formal approach
- Hierarchical structure of decisions
- Use of models and planning frameworks
- Distinct steps
- Chief Executive responsible for the whole process whilst operational managers are separately responsible for implementation
- Strategies are detailed and explicit

### Emergent Strategy Approach

- Development of strategy is an iterative process
- Decisions are smaller and may be taken anywhere in the organization
- These small decisions take shape until they form an articulated strategy
- This approach implies both empowerment and the ability to undertake systematic analysis throughout the organization

## Strategic decision making in SMEs

Small and Medium sized Enterprises (SMEs) have particular issues and, therefore, adopt appropriate responses

| **Issues** |
| --- |
| ■ Limited resources: |
| ◇ Time |
| ◇ Finance |
| ◇ Professional expertise |
| ■ Often no 'team of functional experts' |
| ■ The Managing Director may have sole responsibility for Strategic Marketing Decisions |

| **Responses** |
| --- |
| ■ Emergent approach to decision making |
| ■ Creation of 'Virtual Organizations' |
| ■ Relationships: |
| ◇ *Inform* strategy development |
| ◇ *Add form* to the strategy |

## Revision tips

■ Strategic Decisions are based on developing and leveraging sustainable sources of competitive advantage. These are, however, often affected by changes in the macro or micro environment, including the actions of competitors and the expectations of customers

■ This unit focuses on the need and reasons for continual review of environmental changes and consequent challenge of extant thinking within an organization

■ Identify the global and local drivers that affect sources of competitive advantage, together with competitive actions that do the same

■ Consider how organizations should respond to these changes by developing innovative strategies

■ This response may be achieved by adopting a less formal approach to planning, allowing emergent strategies to be considered alongside formally planned strategies. This may, of course, require and appropriate change in the culture of the organization

■ Finally, remember that the ultimate aim of Strategic Decisions is to deliver value to shareholders and, in order to achieve this, must deliver value to other stakeholder groups as well, particularly customers

# COMPETITIVE STRATEGY AS A LEARNING PROCESS

Unit 3

➡ Explore competitive marketing strategy as an emergent/learning process
➡ Examine the role of knowledge management in sustaining competitive advantage
➡ Evaluate the incorporation of customer-led internet marketing into marketing strategies
➡ Appreciate the value of effective knowledge management in creating competitive advantage

**Syllabus Reference: 2.7–2.9, 3.9**

## Learning and knowledge management

■ In order to make effective decisions, managers must have access to information on which to base them. Knowledge must, therefore, be both acquired ('learning') and processed and distributed to those who need it ('managing')

■ Information must be acquired, which is not necessarily a learning process in this case, and managed

**Market orientation** – The presence of a culture within an organization, which is focused towards the understanding of customer and competitors and so can create superior value for consumers.

**Learning organization** – An organization that has an effective learning capability and is able to efficiently manage its knowledge base to re-orient strategies and respond to competitive challenges and so reshape themselves to sustain their competitiveness.

**Signal learning** – Signal learning is concerned with monitoring the environment and the signalling of challenges and changes in a firm's markets and its performance in that market.

**3R learning** – The 3Rs stand for reflect, re-evaluate and respond. 3R learning occurs in anticipation of, and in response to, critical events occurring in a firm's markets. It is this type of learning that firms that successfully reinvent themselves undergo in reflecting on the demise of their traditional basis for competitive advantage.

**Knowledge management** – The systematic management of the knowledge gained through rigorous approach to the research and analysis undertaken. To make effective strategic decisions, it is of paramount importance that the knowledge built is trustworthy, credible and verifiable and that it is accessible to all the managers involved in the decision-making process.

## Competitive strategy as an emergent learning process

Sustainable competitive advantage is built on the ability to adapt to changing market conditions and so make effective decisions to develop and implement a strategy which delivers superior value to customers. Learning is required to acquire and develop the skills to do this.

Wilson and Gilligan (2004) suggest the following elements of a **customer value-based philosophy**:

- A strong market orientation
- A process of continuous learning
- A commitment to innovation

### Organizational values for effective learning

- A commitment to learning
- Open mindedness
- A shared vision
- Organizational knowledge sharing

| High and satisfactory performance levels | A contentment with the organization's achievements and position | **The inability to escape the past** | A build up of resources | The emergence of the belief that resources/size can substitute for creativity |
| --- | --- | --- | --- | --- |
| Deeply etched recipes within the organization | A vulnerability to new rules of competition | **The inability to invent the future** | A failure to reinvent leadership | Momentum/ action is mistaken for leadership and strategy |

## Knowledge management informing strategy

### The macro environment

- Identification of SLEPT factors that affect an organization's environment
- Evaluation of the impact that these factors will have on the organization including buyer behaviour and ability to supply

### Industry/market analysis

- Identification of industry and geographical boundaries
- Identification and effect of stakeholders
- Impact of Porter's 5 Forces on the industry

### Competitor analysis

- Identification of current and potential competitors within your present and future markets
- Identification of their strengths, weaknesses, and intentions
- Identification of their response patterns to competition

### Customer analysis

- Who they are and what they buy
- Who is involved in their decisions
- Why and how do they purchase
- When, where and how often do they purchase

# Revision tips

■ This unit deals with the ability of organizations to both learn and develop processes to manage that learning and the outcomes from it

■ Ensure, therefore, that you are familiar with types of learning (Signal and 3R), the type of information that is required on which to base Strategic Decisions relating to competitive strategies and, finally, the processes and systems that must be put in place to support the learning and information management

■ The Internet plays different roles in organizations. In some it is fundamental to their competitive strategy, in others, it has a less important role, possibly simply as a promotional medium. However, even for these organizations, it is important to recognize that competitors may be leveraging its capability more effectively

■ Whilst International Marketing is not treated separately within the syllabus, you should consider the implications of the more complex and uncertain aspects of gathering and managing information on an international or global scale

# DEVELOPING CORPORATE WIDE MARKETING INNOVATION

Unit 4

## LEARNING OUTCOMES

➡ Explain the nature of innovation in marketing and the factors affecting its development in decisions to create competitive advantage and customer preference

➡ Evaluate the role of innovation management and risk-taking in achieving competitive advantage

➡ Examine the issues in creating an innovative marketing culture within an organization

➡ Evaluate the incorporation of customer-led Internet marketing into marketing strategies

**Syllabus Reference: 2.2–2.4, 2.9**

## The nature and impact of innovation

■ In this unit, innovation is examined from a number of perspectives

■ First, the nature of technological innovation is considered, together with the processes necessary to exploit it effectively

■ Following on from this, the implications of bringing new products to the market, utilizing innovative approaches, including the Internet, are considered

■ Finally, the creation of an organizational culture to facilitate innovation is considered

**Diffusion curve** – is the model of the spread of a new product into the markets, split into customer response segments (innovators, early adopters, early majority, late majority and laggards).

**Industry breakpoints** – are defined (Strebel, 1996) as a new offering to the market that is so superior in terms of customer value that it disrupts the rules of the competitive game. Two types of breakpoints are discussed. *Divergent breakpoints* are associated with the sharply increasing variety in the competitive offerings and consequently higher value for the customer. *Convergent breakpoints* are the result of improvements in the system and processes resulting in lower delivered costs.

**Continuous innovations** – cause negligible or slightly disruptive effects upon the purchase and consumption of the product.

**Dynamically continuous innovations** – have a more disruptive effect on the way that the products and services are used.

**Discontinuous innovations** – have a highly disruptive effect upon usage and purchasing patterns and these innovations require a high level of marketing to explain the benefits and to educate consumers about how the product should be used.

# Technology lifecycle and competitive advantage

## Diffusion curve

*Source:* Doole and Lowe: CIM Coursebook *Strategic Marketing Decisions* (Elsevier Butterworth-Heinemann, 2004).

## Opportunity identification

Doole and Lowe (2005) have discussed various techniques to identify opportunities. These include:

- Scientific exploration – that starts with no immediate application or customer benefit in mind
- Analysis of current and anticipated customer needs – is an obvious starting point. Asking customers what they want usually identifies new product and service developments
- Segmenting markets further – than they have been segmented before is an effective way of developing products and services to meet more effectively the needs of subsegments of customers
- Identifying a new emerging segment – that is born out of changes in the mood, attitudes and expectation of customers and dissatisfaction with current offerings
- Applying existing techniques in a new sector – applying a technology, process or technique from one business sector to another
- Vertical integration – of the supply chain creating a new, better value route to market
- Business rationalization – or mergers often lead to some products and services being no longer required or a customer segment no longer being satisfied
- Innovation in mature sectors – innovations have taken place here by offering customers a quantum leap in value

## The innovation process

In respect of product and service innovation, a systematic process is required to:

■ Increase the number of ideas coming forward

■ Better manage the process from idea generation to commercialization

■ Increase the chances of success

■ Screen out potential losing ideas as early as possible in order to avoid wasting effort

■ Minimize the early costs of investigating individual ideas

■ Encourage everyone in the organization to suggest innovations and improvements

■ Increase the speed to market

■ Maximize the value of the innovation

*Source:* Doole and Lowe: CIM Coursebook *Strategic Marketing Decisions* (Elsevier Butterworth-Heinemann, 2004).

# Marketing strategy process innovations

| Innovations | Some examples |
| --- | --- |
| Environmental changes | Responding to legal changes (e.g. safety or environmental pollution regulations, market derogation) |
| | Responding to technological advances |
| Resources and capabilities audit | Exploiting company competencies in a new way (e.g. using e-business) |
| Strategy | Segmenting the market further than it is at present |
| | Repositioning to benefit from changes in customer needs and attitudes |
| Market entry alternatives | Participating in an alliance to redefine the market |
| The marketing mix | Focusing on interactive rather than mass communications |
| Supply chain | Finding new value from supply chain contributions |
| Relationships | Redefining the mix to solution provision, rather than selling products and services |

# Innovation in internet marketing

| Six-Is | Characteristics of the Internet |
| --- | --- |
| Interactivity | Customer initiated contact |
| | Marketer has 100% customer attention |
| Intelligence | Can continuously collect and analyse information and make individually focused offers |
| Individualization | Marketing communications is tailored to meet individual needs so achieving mass customization |
| Integration | Managing integrated external and internal marketing communications and mixed mode buying |
| Industry restructuring | Disintermediation involves removing the traditional intermediaries from the distribution channel |
| | Reintermediation involves gaining a presence on websites that might fulfil the role of intermediary |
| Independence of location | Reach can be extended into countries where it is not viable to locate a significant sales support activity |

## Revision tips

■ Innovation is a frequent theme of Postgraduate Diploma exam questions. Ensure that you are familiar both with the different categories of innovations from 'new to the world breakthroughs' to minor adaptations

■ As well as being familiar with the processes of innovation, consider the organizational implications of creating an environment that nurtures innovation: processes, resources, reward systems and organizational attitude and culture

■ Remember that innovation extends to embrace far more than simply products and services. Innovative approaches to marketing strategy applied to both new and existing products and services can deliver enhanced value to an organization

■ Finally ensure that you are familiar with the ways in which the Internet can affect the whole of an organization's innovation strategy, from facilitating information gathering, through adding value to product to new distribution and promotional approaches

# DEVELOPING CORPORATE WIDE MARKETING INNOVATION

Unit 5

➡ Evaluate Porter's three generic strategies in the context of today's competitive environment.

➡ Critically appraise strategic marketing decisions for pioneers, challengers, followers and niche players

➡ Identify and critically evaluate strategic options in relation to shareholder value, using appropriate decision tools

➡ Describe the formulation and evaluation of competitive strategies

**Syllabus Reference: 3.2–3.5**

## Evaluating and developing strategy

■ In the face of a continually changing environment in which the bases of competitive advantage are not only changing with time, but also vary across markets which have differing lifecycles, organizations must make positive decisions to avoid strategic drift

■ These decisions will rest on adopting generic competitive and targeting & positioning strategies that are appropriate both to the market opportunities and also to the organization's competitive stance or market position (e.g. Leader, Challenger, Follower etc.)

## KEY DEFINITIONS

### Five definitions of strategy

*Strategies can be intended*

1. **Strategy as a plan** – a consciously intended course of action.

2. **Strategy as a play** – just a specific manoeuvre to outwit rivals.

*Strategies can be realized through behaviour*

3. **Strategy as a pattern** – a stream of consistent behaviours, whether intended or not. It is worth comparing strategic intent with strategic reality. Strategic intent is often only partially realized in the form of a delivered strategy (the reality). There is often an unrealized part of this strategy, which leaves gaps that are often filled by emergent strategies that are not part of the initial intentions.

*Strategy can be about external focus*

4. **Strategy as a position** – a unique location for the organization within its environment achieved by matching up the organization (internal context) with the environment (external context).

*Strategy can also be an internal focus*

5. **Strategy as a perspective** – an ingrained way of perceiving the world.

*Source:* Mintzberg *et al.,* 2003

# Strategy evaluation: the reasons for marketing strategy failure and wear-out

- Poor general management and inability to implement an appropriate strategy:
    - ◇ Operational inefficiency
    - ◇ Lack of investment
    - ◇ Poor leadership
- An inability to cope with market changes:
    - ◇ Economic and sector lifecycles
    - ◇ Legislative and technological changes
    - ◇ Slower than expected growth or diffusion
    - ◇ Distribution channels

- Ineffective marketing management:
    - ◇ Ineffective use of marketing tools and resources
    - ◇ Emergence of competitive innovation or new competitors
    - ◇ Overdependence on one customer or product
- Removal of a protected environment:
    - ◇ End of a monopoly
    - ◇ Change of customer needs
    - ◇ Lack of customer and competitor focus

## Alternative marketing approaches

**Product push marketing** – is an approach that concentrates on persuading customers to buy the products and services that the firm can produce, deliver and further develop easily, largely using their existing realm of knowledge and resources

**Customer-led marketing** – is typified by those organizations that do everything they can to satisfy customer needs. Some organizations have taken this to extremes and set out to deliver customer needs almost irrespective of cost

**Resource-based marketing** – is considered to be a balanced strategy between meeting the market requirements and exploiting the organization's capabilities to serve the market. Resource-based marketing takes into account the competitive situation, the full range of assets, skills and competencies of the organization and aims to exploit the organization's role within the supply chain

**Entrepreneurial marketing** – Entrepreneurs tend to focus on the opportunity or market gap, irrespective of whether or not this will make use of existing assets and resources. Entrepreneurial marketing usually takes the form of a new business start or a new spin out from within an existing firm

**Network marketing** – is becoming increasingly significant as organizations, desperate for growth, use connections through alliances, partnerships and equity participation in other organizations to exploit opportunities that are not deliverable through their directly owned assets

## Criteria for a successful strategy

- Clear decisive objectives: although subordinate goals may change in the heat of the campaign or competition, the overriding goals must remain clear and understood

- Maintaining the initiative: it must allow freedom of action, enhance commitment and maintain the pace and determine the course of events, rather than reacting to them

- Concentration: it must be capable of concentrating superior power at a particular place and time to be decisive

- Flexibility: it must keep in reserve resources and capabilities in order to allow flexibility and manoeuvrability

- Co-ordinated and committed leadership: leaders must be appointed for each of the goals, and their interests and ambitions must match the needs of their roles

- Surprise: it must make use of speed, secrecy and intelligence to attack unprepared competitors

- Security: it must secure resources to support the actions

## Competitive stances

The first three categories are discussed by Wilson and Gilligan under the terminology of competitive position; Doole and Lowe add two further categories of Pioneers and Market Nichers:

*Leaders* – keep ahead of the field by developing an ever-stronger selling proposition and competitive advantage to build customer loyalty, discouraging other possible market entrants

*Challengers* – develop a strong alternative proposition and challenge the leader's weaknesses continually, often by aggressive pricing

*Followers* – imitate the other competitors at lower prices. They look for unexploited opportunities

*Pioneers* – innovators who tend to be first into new opportunities. Some may also be market leaders but others may not maintain a consistent strategy and may fail to consolidate their pioneering efforts and build their businesses

*Market Nichers* – survive and grow through specializing in a part of the market that is too small to be attractive to larger firms or in a market niche that they define and create themselves. With globalization, some market nichers have built substantial businesses through creating a global niche

# Revision tips

■ The redefinition of strategy is central to this module and it is vital for exam success to understand clearly the fundamentals of this area

■ Opportunities in each market segment should be matched against the assets and competencies of the organization and prioritized by the suitability of the strategic fit to achieving the organization's objectives

■ In doing so, a number of factors should be considered, including the generic basis of competition in that segment (Cost Leadership, Focus or Differentiation) and Competitive Stance. The latter, especially, is a recurring theme in CIM Postgraduate examinations

■ Strategies may then be tested against other criteria, including acceptability to stakeholders, feasibility and sustainability

■ A suitable positioning for each targeted segment may then be developed and implemented

■ Alternative approaches to developing strategies are appropriate to different types of organizations. In these cases, the organizations must nurture the capability to develop strategies using these approaches and must ensure that processes, skills and knowledge are managed appropriately at relevant levels within the organization

# STRATEGIC DECISIONS FOR GLOBAL DEVELOPMENT

## LEARNING OUTCOMES

➡ Examine the issues of decisions to build competitive capability and approaches to leveraging capability to create advantage across geographically diverse markets

➡ Determine the lessons of best practice from strategic decisions made by successful global companies

➡ Leverage individual and corporate learning across geographically diverse markets for competitive advantage

**Syllabus Reference: 3.1, 3.6, 3.10**

## International and global marketing

There are two major differences between national and international/global marketing:

- Self-evidently, international marketing is inherently **more complex** than national marketing. Not only are there more variables to manage, the level of uncertainty may be higher as information is less reliable

- Although the vast majority of organizations are involved in international marketing because they face international competition, the **extent of internationalization** of their operations is within their own control. It is, therefore, a strategic decision that organizations have to make

## KEY DEFINITIONS

**Export marketing** – The marketing of goods and/or services across national/political boundaries.

**Multinational marketing** – The marketing activities of an organization which has activities, interests or operations in more than one country and where there is some kind of influence of control of marketing activities from outside the country in which the goods or services will actually be sold, but where the global markets are primarily perceived to be independent markets and profit centres in their own right.

**Global marketing** – Where the whole organization focuses on the selection and exploitation of global marketing opportunities and marshals resources around the globe with the objective of achieving a global competitive advantage.

## Drivers of globalization

- **Increased market access** as markets in China, Central and Eastern Europe are opened up
- **Increased market opportunities** because of the deregulation of many markets
- **Greater uniformity of industry standards**, encouraged, for example, by the EU sourcing of products and services from a wider range of countries, particularly those emerging markets with a high ratio of skills to cost
- **More globally standardized products and services**
- **Common technology** used in many more markets, particularly markets where there is a high cost of R&D that must be recovered through sales in many countries
- Similar customer requirements leading to **transnational customer segments**
- Competition from the same organizations in each major market and thus **interdependence of markets**
- **Cooperation between organizations** from different parts of the world, leading to companies competing and cooperating with each other in the same markets
- Worldwide or regional **organization of distribution**, ignoring country boundaries
- **Communication** generated and received almost anywhere in the world
- Global organization strategies that increasingly treat the world as **one market**

# Strategy alternatives for global firms

## Leveraging capability in global markets

The **benefits for a firm** are increasing its scale of operations through increased global activity. They include:

- Better knowledge of the requirements and expectations of customers worldwide

- The economies associated with increased scale of operations and R&D

- Improving efficiency and effectiveness through repeating programmes and processes and, as a result . . .

- Building the capability and knowledge of the organization that can be applied to new business and marketing initiatives

These benefits are best achieved through **Programme and Process Standardization**. Note, however:

- The standardization of programmes will achieve the benefit of lower costs

- Standardization of programmes may not be advisable because of differences in market conditions and culture. Organizations should, therefore, decide on the degree of programme standardization that is appropriate

- Standardization of processes is more desirable because it not only enables savings to be made but also facilitates corporate learning.

# International marketing challenges

Firms face a number of critical strategic decisions and issues of implementation in achieving best practice in International Marketing:

**Opportunity analysis and marketing research** – are essential to decide which countries are most commercially attractive, offer the most potential and can most effectively be served by the company

**Sensitivity to different cultures** – is essential throughout the process, including customer research, product and service development, and communications

**Transnational segmentation** – Over-focus on country characteristics segmentation rather than transnational benefit segmentation can seriously curtail global development because of the failure to benefit from scale economies. Good practice requires a hierarchy approach starting with transnational segmentation followed then by country-based segmentation

**Market entry strategies** – Arguably the most critical decision for organizations is deciding which market entry strategy to adopt

**Marketing mix** – There are a series of decisions about the marketing mix, the level of standardization that is possible and adaptation to local market needs that is necessary. Decisions are required on the product portfolio, new product development, distribution, communications and pricing strategy, and each of these are critical. Decisions are influenced by different factors, including the stage of economic development, cultural demands, legal controls, usage conditions and ethical considerations

## The geographic development of SMEs

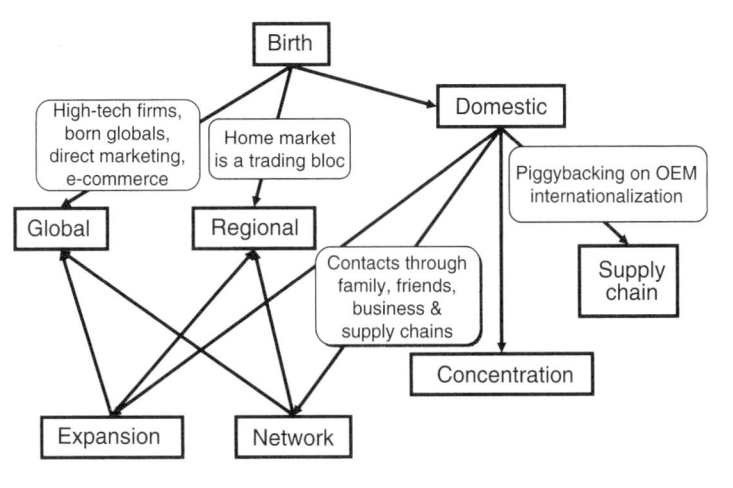

*Source:* Doole and Lowe: CIM Coursebook *Strategic Marketing Decisions* (Elsevier Butterworth-Heinemann, 2004)

# The importance of niche marketing

|  | Exporting | International niche marketing |
|---|---|---|
| Marketing strategy | Selling production capacity | Meeting customer needs |
| Financial objective | To amortize overheads | To add value |
| Segmentation | Usually by country and customer characteristics | By identifying common international customer benefit |
| Pricing | Cost based | Market or customer based |
| Management focus | Efficiency in operations | Meeting market requirements |
| Distribution | Using existing agents or distributors | Managing the supply chain |
| Market information | Relying on agent or distributor feedback | Analysing the market situation and customer needs |
| Customer relationship | Working through intermediaries | Building multiple level relationships |

## Leveraging learning in SMEs

SMEs can be characterized by their proactivity in international marketing and can be categorized as passive, reactive, experimental, proactive or world-class international marketers as shown below.

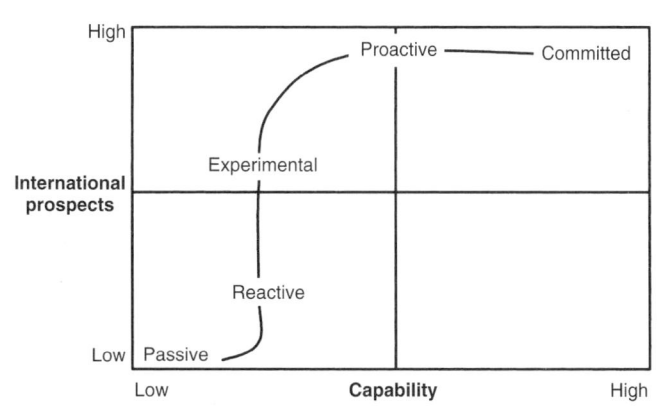

*Source:* Doole and Lowe: CIM Coursebook *Strategic Marketing Decisions* (Elsevier Butterworth-Heinemann, 2004)

# Revision tips

■ There are strong drivers for globalization resulting in pressure on organizations to operate internationally in some way

■ Recognizing the challenges in doing so, organizations have to make a fundamental strategic decision as to whether or not to adopt an international strategy

■ In addition to economies of scale, there are many other benefits of operating internationally. An important benefit is being able to leverage both capability and corporate learning across global markets

■ A range of opportunities has been opened up for SMEs. In order to take advantage of these, SMEs have to sustain and develop niche markets

# INNOVATIVE STRATEGIES FOR FAST GLOBAL GROWTH

Unit 7

**LEARNING OUTCOMES**

➡ Evaluate the use of e-technology to build and exploit competitive advantage
➡ Critically appraise innovative marketing strategies in small and large companies operating on global markets

Syllabus Reference: 3.7, 3.8

## Entrepreneurial and hypergrowth businesses

■ This unit examines the strategies developed by firms that have successfully met the challenges of achieving above average performance discussed in Units 2 and 3

■ Hypergrowth businesses are those businesses that have grown at more than 100% over the last three years. This unit discusses how this may be achieved

■ Organizations may be classified along a spectrum as: Pioneers, Second-in, Imitators or Defensive Firms according to their attitude to innovation

**Assets** – are the 'things' that the organization possesses, including the physical facilities, the customer database and brand.

**Competencies** – are skills that exist within the organization's staff, including brand management, IT and supply chain.

**Core competencies** – are the skills that pervade the organization and are those areas and activities in which the firm has a very high-developed ability.

## Competitive advantage

Wilson and Gilligan (2004) suggest that above average performance may be achieved by giving customers exceptional value.

| Product differentiation advantages | Cost advantages |
|---|---|
| ○ Superior quality | ○ Consistent investment in R&D |
| ○ Superior levels of service | ○ High levels of process technology and production efficiency |
| ○ Strong brand names | ○ Patents |
| ○ High levels of brand loyalty | ○ Access to scarce or low cost resources |
| ○ Distribution strengths | ○ Vertical integration |
| ○ High cost to the customer of switching | ○ Distribution efficiency |

# Implementation – the drivers of entrepreneurial companies

Strategic Decisions relating to resource allocation have to be made:

|  | Low (Organizational performance) | High (Organizational performance) |
|---|---|---|
| **Low** (Importance within the market place) | Low priorities | Rethink the effort – customers do not consider this important |
| **High** (Importance within the market place) | Focus for more management effort to strengthen position | Fully resource to maintain current high levels of effort |

Organizational performance: Low — High

*Source:* Doole and Lowe: CIM Coursebook *Strategic Marketing Decisions* (Elsevier Butterworth-Heinemann, 2004)

## Fast growth businesses

Fast growth businesses focus on high levels of **customer management**:

- Segmentation and sub-segmentation
- Understanding lifetime value of customers
- Exploiting cross-selling opportunities
- Managing customers through the whole buying process
- Building relationships with all stakeholders that influence decisions
- Focusing on providing the highest levels of service

The **characteristics** of hypergrowth businesses are that they:

- Focus on being unique and offering exceptional customer value
- Define and exploit a defensible niche
- Have 'leading edge' products and services
- Lead in competitor and performance bench-marking
- Compete in areas that require speed, flexibility and exceptional customer service
- Diversify into related products and adjacent markets
- Leave the industry before the window of opportunity closes

# Beyond customer led

*Source:* Doole and Lowe: CIM Coursebook *Strategic Marketing Decisions* (Elsevier Butterworth-Heinemann, 2004)

## e-Business

e-Business has become an important element in achieving fast growth for all companies and has enabled many small companies to reach larger markets than they would have otherwise done.

Chaffey et al. suggest four Internet business models:

- Business to Business (B2B)
- Business to Consumer (B2C)
- Consumer to Consumer (C2C)
- Consumer to Business (C2B)

In reality, the last of these is a model by which consumers form buying consortia to purchase from businesses.

Doole and Lowe suggest four categories of websites:

- To provide organization information (e.g. www.philips.com)
- Site to provide service online (e.g. www.fedex.com)
- Site to provide information online (e.g. www.bbc.com)
- Site to carry out business transactions (e.g. www.expedia.com)

# Revision tips

- In order for organizations to achieve fast growth, market opportunities for fast growth must be available in an industry, market conditions must be conducive to fast growth and the organization must have the necessary assets and competencies to take advantage of the situation

- The availability of the Internet has created more fast growth opportunities and also brought about more conducive market conditions

- In order to achieve fast growth, the organization's competencies are likely to include a dynamic and entrepreneurial approach to management

- Having embarked on fast growth strategies, organizations must focus on effective management of their product and service portfolio taking particular note of competitor strategies

# BUILDING PORTFOLIO VALUE: BRANDING, PRODUCTS AND SERVICES

Unit 8

## LEARNING OUTCOMES

➡ Explain and evaluate the contribution of value-based marketing

➡ Assess the nature and dimensions of branding/brand decisions, their role in the development of advantage and their significance in global markets

**Syllabus Reference: 4.1, 4.2**

## Products and brands

This unit addresses two important topic areas. The first is the management of an organization's portfolio of products through their lifecycle and the lifecycle of the markets that they serve. This will involve the building and maintenance of the portfolio, including rationalization, where necessary, and the enhancement of products with added value services.

The second topic is that of branding. Brands are intangible assets which create value for both organizations and their customers. As with products, they must be carefully managed in order to leverage their value and avoid erosion of that value.

**A successful brand** – is an identifiable product, service or place augmented in such a way that the buyer or user perceives relevant, unique, sustainable added values that match their needs most closely (de Chernatony, 2001).

**Product portfolio** – is the collection of products and services that are managed together rather than as individual products.

**Brand equity** – is the net present value of the future cash flow attributable to the brand name.

**Intangible assets** – non-material assets such as technical expertise, brands or patents.

## Brands

**Customer Brand Perception**

Formed by:

- **Experience** of previous use
- **Personal referral** from friends etc. Also **peer pressure**
- **Editorial** and other public sources
- **Communications** by the organization, both through promotion and staff/customer interaction

**Categories of Brands**

Categorized by Doyle (2000) as:

- **Attribute brands** which build customer confidence through functional attributes
- **Aspirational brands** that convey to the customers images about the type of people who purchase the brand, so delivering status, recognition and esteem
- **Experience brands** which focus on shared philosophy between customer and brand

Note also the Country of Origin (COO) effect, which, when used correctly, creates trust in the brand.

# Brands

## Benefits to the Organization

Brands can add value to an organization by providing the following benefits (Doyle, 2000):

- Price premium
- Higher volumes
- Lower costs
- Better asset utilization

## Brand Value Erosion

The following factors can lead to the erosion of brand value:

- Private branding
- Brand forgery
- Negative Brand Associations
- Unacceptable business practices
- Unexpected crises
- Grey marketing

## New product and service development

New products and services may fall into a number of categories, as shown in the opposite table. It is important that decisions to commit time and resources to new developments are made in the context of the marketing strategy. In this respect, the questions on the following page need to be answered.

| Category | Contribution |
| --- | --- |
| New to the world | 10% |
| New product lines | 20% |
| Additions to product lines | 26% |
| Revisions/improvements | 26% |
| Cost reductions | 11% |
| Repositionings | 7% |

# New product and service development

| | |
|---|---|
| Fit with mission | Will all stakeholders understand the new idea? |
| Fit with product/market scope | Can the ideas be contained within an identified and easily communicated area? |
| Match between growth strategies and resources | Are the resources being used effectively within the growth options? |
| Delivery of competitive advantage | Is the advantage tangible or in the mind of the innovator? |
| Synergy between firm and target market | Will this add value to the current customer segment? |
| Fit with positioning | Does this reinforce or enhance the current positioning? Does it fit with the brand image? |
| Market entry alternatives | Could the idea be better exploited by alternative collaboration in order to reduce risks? |
| Is the timing right? | Should the product be launched now or should the firm wait for others to create the demand? |

## Revision tips

■ The review of an organization's product and service portfolio involves a number of the most important strategic decisions that the organization will make. Products and services should not be viewed in isolation but in the context of the whole portfolio and the organization's business and marketing strategies

■ In an international and global environment, markets may be at different stages of their lifecycles and, for this and other reasons, products and services may be varied from market to market

■ Brands add significant value to organizations. This is often intangible and not shown on the balance sheet

■ There are a number of ways in which brands may be valued. One of these is to base the valuation on the net present value of future cashflows attributable to the brand name

■ Brands should be managed through their lifecycle, paying particular attention to the brand naming strategy (referred to as ''Brand Form'' by some writers) and strategies, including innovation and promotion, to build, reposition and extend brands. It may also be necessary to rationalize brands from time to time

# INTEGRATED COMMUNICATIONS AND RELATIONSHIP DEVELOPMENT

## LEARNING OUTCOMES

➡ Evaluate the role of integrated marketing communications in competitive global strategy

➡ Understand the concept of relationship marketing and the role of long-term customer relationships in creating and delivering value

➡ Determine the importance of managing marketing relationships in generating customer commitment

**Syllabus Reference: 4.4–4.6**

## The role and purpose of communications

An organization can achieve competitive advantage by dint of the quality of its relationship with its stakeholders and an integrated strategy for communications is an important aspect of doing so. This unit deals with:

■ The purpose of communications in presenting and exchanging appropriate messages with stakeholders in a way that is integrated across the organization

■ The role of communications in building and supporting relationships with an organization's stakeholders

## KEY DEFINITIONS

**Integrated Marketing Communications** – Shimp (2003) provides a definition of IMC which focuses on five features:

1. Start with the customer or prospect.

2. Use any form of relevant contact.

3. Achieve synergy through consistency across the communication elements.

4. Build relationships.

5. Affect behaviour.

**Relationship marketing** – is creating and building mutually beneficial relationships by bringing together the necessary stakeholders and resources to deliver the best possible perceived value proposition for the customer.

# Internal, interactive and external marketing

**Internal marketing**
Communicating to the staff, the mission, values, objectives, priorities and procedures

**The company**

**External marketing**
Ensuring that the range of services, pricing structure, promotional effort and location meet external stakeholder expectations

**Staff**

**Customer groups**

**Interactive marketing**
The effectiveness with which staff deal with each of the customer groups

*Source:* Doole and Lowe: CIM Coursebook *Strategic Marketing Decisions* (Elsevier Butterworth-Heinemann, 2004)

## Four levels of communications and relationship building

*Source:* Doole and Lowe CIM Coursebook *Strategic Marketing Decisions* (Elsevier Butterworth-Heinemann, 2004)

# The integration of communications

An organization communicates in eight ways
(Davidson (2002)):

- Actions
- Behaviour
- Face-to-face by management
- Signals, from the organization's actions, facilities and objects
- Product and services, especially their quality levels
- Intended communications
- Word of mouth and mouse
- Comment by other organizations

---

**The areas of integration**

**Corporate Strategy** for internal and external stakeholders. Values, culture, policies, objectives, standards and style

**Brand Strategies** for customers. Consistent messages to communicate what the brand stands for.

**Global Integration.** Whilst consistency of communications is essential and standardization is desirable, there are pitfalls in over-standardization.

**Marketing Mix Integration.** Customers receive communications from every element of the marketing mix, both intended and unintended.

# Barriers to effective communication

### Within the organization's control:

- Inconsistency in the messages conveyed to customers by staff at different levels, in different locations

- Different styles of presentation of corporate identity, brand and product image

- A lack of co-ordination of messages

- Failure to appreciate the differences in the fields of perception of the sender and receiver

- Ignoring the needs of different audiences

- Achieving little impact from a single message

- Lack of synergy and reinforcement from multiple communications

- More than one message communicated together, so confusing the recipient

- Setting unclear objectives

- Trying to achieve too much with one communication to justify the high cost

- Inconsistency within the distribution channel

- Advertising agencies focusing on their creative work rather than selling the product

### Problems outside the organization's control include:

- Counterfeiting or other infringements of patents

- Grey marketing, which is distribution through channels that are not authorized by the organization

- Competitors, governments or pressure groups attack the standards and values of organizations by alleging, fairly or unfairly, bad business practice

# Marketing communications planning

| | |
|---|---|
| **S**ituation analysis | Environment market: stakeholders, competition, customers, structure |
| **O**bjectives | The short- and long-term objectives |
| **M**essages | Target audiences and messages |
| **C**ommunications | The media, the promotions mix and integration of the channels |
| **B**udgets | Basis of allocation |
| **C**ontrol | Measurement, evaluation and correct deviations |

| | |
|---|---|
| Users | Often initiate the purchase and define the specification |
| Influencers | Help define the product and evaluate the alternatives |
| Deciders | Decide product requirements and suppliers |
| Approvers | Authorize the proposals of deciders and buyers |
| Buyers | Have the formal authority for selecting suppliers and negotiating terms |
| Gatekeepers | Can stop the sellers reaching the buying centre |

# Communication tools and media

## Media – Terminology

**Reach** is the percentage of the target audience exposed to the message at least once during the relevant period

**Coverage** is the size of the potential audience that might be exposed to a potential medium

**Frequency** is the repetition level of the communication

**Gross Rating Point (GRP)** is the reach multiplied by the frequency and is a measure of the total number of exposures

**Efficiency** is reaching as many customers as possible given a constant budget

**Recency** as a concept suggests that potential customers must be reached when they are ready to buy

## The Communications Tools

**Advertising** is a one way communication whose role can be to inform, persuade, remind and reinforce

**Sales promotion** is a short term means of increasing sales

**PR** is perceived as "news" and so more credible than advertising. A key role is in managing crises

**Sponsorship** is also a form of PR

**Personal selling** is a two way means of communication used when complex negotiations and persuasion are needed

**Direct marketing** is a means of communication that tries to elicit a response from the customer. This is increasingly becoming a key part of a Relationship strategy

# Relationship marketing – objectives

Relationship Marketing focuses on increasing the lifetime value of a customer and the following objectives:

- Maintain and build customers by offering more tailored and cost effective business solutions
- Use existing relationships to obtain referral to other business units and supply chain members
- Increase the revenue from customers by offering solutions that are a combination of products and services
- Reduce the operational and communications cost of servicing the customers, including the work prior to a trading relationship

## Revision tips

- Communication strategies must be integrated with each other, offering consistent message to all stakeholders, and must also be consistent with the objectives and strategies of the organization

- Always consider who the audiences are and how they may be segmented. A stakeholder analysis will allow audiences to be identified in a particular situation

- Internal staff and staff in the extended organization are stakeholders and should be considered in any strategic communications decisions

- Relationship marketing involves the development of a Customer Relationship Management strategy that will involve integrating all aspects of marketing activity to build mutually beneficial relationships between customers, suppliers and other stakeholders

# USING THE EXTENDED ORGANIZATION TO ADD PORTFOLIO VALUE

Unit 10

## LEARNING OUTCOMES

➡ Determine the importance of managing marketing relationships in generating customer commitment

➡ Examine the role of alliances and the creation of competitive advantage through supply chain development and marketing partnerships

➡ Examine how pricing policies and strategies can be used to build competitive advantage

**Syllabus Reference: 4.6–4.8**

## The extended organization

■ This unit deals with two main topics. The first is the concept of the Extended Organization – the linked Value Chains at which level the customer buys. These linked Value Chains comprise both an organization's own value chain and that of its partners' – suppliers and outsourced agencies

■ The second topic is the nature of pricing, its objectives and strategies and its relationship to the cost drivers identified by the Value Chain Analysis

## KEY DEFINITIONS

**The value chain** – is the series of activities that create additional value for customers and comprises the use of materials, tangible and intangible assets.

**A strategic alliance** – is an informal arrangement between two or more organizations to pursue a common objective.

**A joint venture** – is a separate enterprise created using assets from two or more companies who share the equity and risk.

## Porter's value chain

Michael Porter's Value Chain identifies the following primary and supporting activities that comprise the operating model of a simple, production-biased firm.

### *Primary activities:*

- Inbound Logistics
- Operations
- Outbound Logistics
- Marketing and Sales
- Service

### *Secondary activities:*

- The firm's infrastructure
- Human resources management
- Technology development
- Procurement

Doyle (2000) explains the contributions that marketing makes to adding value and helping firms grow through:

- Reducing costs through eliminating duplication and unnecessary processes
- Benefiting from concentrating expertise and complementary activity
- Exploiting new market opportunities
- Reducing investment for organizations through outsourcing rather than manufacturing components
- Enabling small firms to have similar costs to large firms

# Distribution channel management

| Manufacturer best placed to supply | Intermediaries best placed to supply |
| --- | --- |
| • Complex products with continuous development | • Simple product with basic service levels |
| • Made-to-order products | • Standard stocked lines |
| • Where a high level of service and support is required | • Large customer base |
| • Where there is a small customer base | • Smaller customers |
| • Where the transactions are of high volume or value | • Geographically difficult to cover |
| • Easy to cover locations | • Small random deliveries from stock |
| • Where shipments are large scale, planned and just-in-time | • Low level feedback |
| • High level feedback is required | |

# Routes to market

*Source:* Doole and Lowe: CIM Coursebook *Strategic Marketing Decisions* (Elsevier Butterworth-Heinemann, 2004)

## Pricing decisions

- Survival
- Return on investment
- Market stabilization
- Maintenance and improvement of position
- Reflecting product differentiation
- Market skimming
- Market penetration
- Early cash recovery
- Preventing new entry

In responding to price-based competition, organizations should consider the following:

- Whether they are a leader, follower or me too
- Whether they can prevent new entry
- Whether their cost levels offer scope for price cutting
- Whether they, or their competitors, have the resources for a price war
- Whether they are dependent on the product
- Whether they are committed to the market sector
- The potential returns from price cutting
- The distinctiveness of the product and brand loyalty
- Whether a price cut will affect the perception of brand value

# Revision tips

- Remember that channels have a variety of roles and, while disintermediation through using the Internet can save costs, there may be a consequent loss of channel functions and, therefore, a reduction in customer service levels

- The Value Chain is a useful tool for identifying where an organization can add value or save cost. It will, however, be different for different types of organizations

- Linkages between elements of the Value Chain, and the effectiveness of links to the Value Chains of other organizations are important because customers typically buy at the level of the *linked* Value Chains

- In making strategic pricing decisions, it is extremely important to know what factors affect a firm's reaction in the face of a pricing attack. The firm must understand its own objectives, strategies, strengths and weaknesses as well as those of its competitors. It may then decide to maintain or drop prices or, possibly, withdraw from the market altogether

# FINANCIAL APPRAISAL FOR STRATEGIC MARKETING DECISIONS

**Unit 11**

## LEARNING OUTCOMES

➡ Examine the implications of strategic marketing decisions for implementation and control

➡ Apply investment appraisal techniques to marketing investment decisions

➡ Examine alternative approaches to model potential investment decisions in the deployment of marketing resources

➡ Define budgetary and planning control techniques for use in the control of marketing plans and explain the pitfalls of control systems and how they may be overcome

**Syllabus Reference: 5.1, 5.3, 5.4, 5.6**

## Financial measures

■ The ultimate measure of the value of any activity is financial. However, this financial return may be neither immediate nor direct. Ways of measuring the true value of this return must be found in order to justify it.

■ In this unit the way in which added value to a company is measured are considered. Three approaches are evaluated: Cashflow; Economic Value Added (EVA) and Return on Capital Employed (ROCE)

■ In addition, both Cost/Volume/Profit (Breakeven) analysis as a means of supporting short term decisions and ratio analysis, as a measure of performance, are considered

**Return on capital employed** – is a measure commonly used by companies to assess the added value to shareholders resulting from the capital invested.

**Payback** – measures the number of years it will take to recover the original investment from the net cash flows resulting from a project. The method is based on being able to estimate a future flow of funds.

**Cost/Volume/Profit (CVP) analysis** – is used to help a company understand the relationship between volume, costs and profits and used to budget and forecast the break-even point.

**A ratio** – takes two variables (e.g. profit/sales) and compares them with other measures of the same variable in another time period or in another company in order to assess the performance of the company and the efficiency of its operations.

# Financial analysis for long-term decision making

Investment projects may be evaluated based on a number of factors. These include Payback Period and Net Present Value.

The objective of Payback Period is simply to determine how long it will take to recover the investment made from the net profit on that investment.

The objective of the second is to take into account the 'time value of money' in evaluating the investment. The exact timing of the return is required and a Discount Rate (usually given from tables although it is simple to calculate) is applied to each year's net income, resulting in that amount being reduced to reflect the fact that money received now and in the future is worth less than money which is immediately available for reinvestment.

## Payback Period

$$\text{No of years} = \frac{\text{Total Investment}}{\text{Net income per year}}$$

Note that the income may vary each year and so a calculation of the cumulative net income will be required to determine the exact time at which the investment is recovered.

## Net Present Value

The Net Present Value of an income stream is calculated as:

(Income year 1) × (Year 1 Discount Rate)

+ (Income year 2) × (Year 2 Discount Rate)

+ (Income year 3) × (Year 3 Discount Rate) etc.

Now the initial investment can be evaluated depending on whether it is less (☺) or more (☹) than the NPV of the above income stream.

## Assessing owner/shareholder value

One of the main objectives of business is to maximize shareholders' wealth by adding value to the company or organization. Three methods of measuring this Shareholder Added Value are considered.

### Cashflow Valuation

The calculation of cashflow generated by a strategy can be split into two parts:

- Present Value (PV) of Cashflow during the forecast period. Calculated as the PV of the net cashflows (income less expenditure) during the forecast period.

- PV of Cashflow after the period (residual value)

The latter is difficult to attribute to marketing strategies and so they may be evaluated on the basis of the first alone.

### Economic Value Added

This is simply the amount by which the return on an investment exceeds the cost of the capital required for that investment.

EVA = Net Operating Profits After Tax

    − (capital invested

      × weighted average cost of that capital)

The figure in brackets is effectively the return that could have been secured by investing that capital elsewhere.

### Return on Capital Employed (ROCE)

$$ROCE = \frac{\text{Earnings Before Interest and Tax} \times 100\%}{\text{Capital Employed}}$$

Doyle is critical of this measure because the value of earnings (which includes the value of assets) may be arbitrary and subject to risk.

## Cost/volume/profit (CVP) analysis

One of the main functions of CVP Analysis is to enable the Breakeven Point for a product (or range of products) to be calculated. This is the point at which the volume is such that neither a profit or a loss is being made on that product. Above this volume a profit will be made; below it, a loss will be suffered.

$$\text{Breakeven Volume} = \frac{\text{Total Fixed Costs}}{\text{Contribution per unit}}$$

In order to calculate the volume required to make a given level of profit, that profit may be considered as an additional fixed cost. So:

$$\text{Vol required for profit of £NN} = \frac{\text{Total Fixed Costs} + \text{NN}}{\text{Contribution per unit}}$$

| CVP Analysis Definitions | |
|---|---|
| Fixed Costs | Costs that do not vary with production volume |
| Variable Costs | Costs that do vary with production volume |
| Contribution per unit | Sales Revenue per unit minus Variable Costs per unit |
| Margin of safety % | The percentage by which sales would have to fall before a loss is made. A measure of risk. |
| Contribution Sales Ratio | $\dfrac{\text{Selling Price} - \text{Variable Cost}}{\text{Selling Price}}$ |
| Profit Volume ratio | $\dfrac{\text{Sales Revenue} - \text{Total Variable Costs}}{\text{Sales Revenue}}$ |

# Financial techniques for evaluating performance

Ratio analysis is useful for showing trends over a period of time and for enabling companies to compare their performance with that of other companies in similar industries.

## Profitability Ratios

Gross Profit Margin $\quad \dfrac{\text{Gross Profit} \times 100\%}{\text{Sales Turnover}}$

Net Profit Margin $\quad \dfrac{\text{Net Profit} \times 100\%}{\text{Sales Turnover}}$

## Sales Ratios

Stock Turnover $\quad \dfrac{\text{Annual Cost of Goods Sold}}{\text{Average Stock Value}}$

NB: This figure is expressed as the number of times/year

## Operational Ratios

Current Ratio $\quad$ Current assets : Current liabilities

Quick Ratio $\quad$ (Current assets − Stock) : Current Liabilities

Debt Collection Period $\quad \dfrac{\text{Debtors}}{\text{Credit sales}/365}$

Creditor Payment Period $\quad \dfrac{\text{Creditors}}{\text{Credit Purchases}/365}$

# Revision tips

- Investment Decisions relate to the comparison of an investment (often initial) to the income or savings accruing as a result of that investment over a period of time. The comparison may be done on a payback, NPV or, possibly, an accounting rate of return basis

- Investments in individual marketing campaigns may be evaluated on the same basis

- Short-term decisions, typically at product or product group level, will be based on techniques such as breakeven analysis

- To track performance of decisions after they have been made, ratio analysis is an appropriate tool for identifying and tracking trends and also for making comparisons with similar organizations operating in the similar markets

# ACHIEVING A SUSTAINABLE COMPETITIVE ADVANTAGE

Unit 12

## LEARNING OUTCOMES

➡ Assess the issues of corporate and social responsibility (CSR), sustainability and ethics in achieving competitive advantage, enhancing corporate reputation and creating stakeholder value

➡ Explain the concept of, and evaluate methods such as balanced scorecard for, stakeholder value measurement

➡ Define performance measurement systems for the deployment of marketing assets and the implementation of marketing plans

➡ Define budgetary and planning control techniques for use in the control of marketing plans and explain the pitfalls of control systems and how they may be overcome

**Syllabus Reference: 4.10, 5.2, 5.5, 5.6**

## Measuring performance

In order for an organization to make effective decisions, the contribution of strategic marketing decisions themselves must be capable of being demonstrated to be effective. This unit addresses:

■ The approaches a manager can take to develop efficient and effective control systems

■ The development of a process through which stakeholder value can be measured

■ The process by which the performance of a marketing program can be critically evaluated

■ The issues and role of Corporate Social Responsibility in sustaining competitive advantage and creating shareholder value by enhancing reputation

## KEY DEFINITIONS

**Evaluation and control mechanisms** – set standards to which marketing strategies should aspire, measure performance and take corrective action when the measurement varies from the level of performance required.

**The Balanced Scorecard** – is a management system to measure current performance and to set priorities for future performance. It incorporates four perspectives: financial perspective, the customer perspective, the internal business perspective and the innovation and learning perspective.

**Corporate social responsibility** – is the term used to describe the level of awareness shown by companies of their social responsibility and the values exhibited with regard to the societal impact of strategic marketing decisions.

## Approaches to measuring performance

In order for marketing to be properly represented at board level, its contribution to profitability and shareholder value must be capable of being demonstrated. This is done by establishing sound control systems and performance metrics.

### Objectives of Control Systems

- To set standards to which marketing strategies should aspire
- To measure performance in a meaningful way
- To assess areas of strengths and weaknesses in marketing programmes
- To establish mechanisms for taking corrective action when required

### Performance Metrics

- **What** are they going to measure
- What are the **organizational mechanisms** for the measuring activities:
  - ◇ Benchmarking
  - ◇ Annual Budgeting procedures
  - ◇ Auditing
- How to ensure performance is measured against **a balanced range of goals and objectives**, for example, those of the balanced scorecard:
  - ◇ Financial
  - ◇ Customers
  - ◇ Internal Business
  - ◇ Innovation and Learning Perspective

## Stakeholders

Stakeholders can be classified into six groups (Doyle, 2000):

- Shareholders/owners
- Employees
- Managers
- Customers
- Suppliers
- Community and Society

# The Balanced Scorecard Kaplan and Norton (1992)

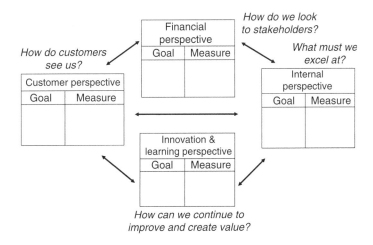

## Ethics and corporate social responsibility

Many companies and professional bodies have codes of ethics and are also regulated by consumer watchdogs and ombudsmen as well as by law.

In addition, companies can differentiate themselves from competitors by dint of their position on Corporate Social Responsibility (CSR). Whilst some companies may simply react or take a defensive position on CSR, others have succeeded in building competitive advantages on a proactive positioning towards CSR by sharing the values of their stakeholders. The societal marketing concept is based on enhancing the well-being of society as well as that of the consumers and shareholders.

# Revision tips

- It is expected that Strategic Decisions will be subject to evaluation. The approach and processes that you recommend to this evaluation are an important element of strategic decision making

- In making Strategic Decisions, you should, there-fore, consider both how they will be evaluated (in terms of process) and, equally importantly, the bases on which they will be evaluated

- Strategic Decisions may be evaluated on a strictly short-term basis. However, in order to demonstrate that they increase shareholder value, their implications in terms of improving, or putting in place the capabilities to improve, customer value should also be considered. Kaplan and Norton's Balanced Scorecard provides one mechanism to achieve this

- The ethical and CSR implications of Strategic Decisions should also be considered. In particular, an organization should understand clearly its stance on ethics and CSR, whether it be defensive or reactive, or whether it seeks to align itself with the values of its stakeholders and so achieve a competitive advantage in doing so. In the latter case, its mission, objectives, strategy and marketing programmes should be consistent with this stance